EVERY QUILTER'S
Foundation Piecing
REFERENCE TOOL

Jane Hall & Dixie Haywood

Publisher: **Amy Marson**

Creative Director: **Gailen Runge**

Acquisitions Editor: **Jan Grigsby**

Editors: **Lisa Ruble and Stacy Chamness**

Technical Editors: **Helen Frost and Amanda Siegfried**

Copyeditor/Proofreader: **Wordfirm Inc.**

Cover Designer/Book Designer: **Kristen Yenche**

Page Layout Artist: **Rose Sheifer-Wright**

Production Coordinator: **Tim Manibusan**

Illustrator: **Tim Manibusan**

Photography by **Christina Carty-Francis and Diane Pedersen** of C&T Publishing, Inc., unless otherwise noted

Library of Congress Cataloging-in-Publication Data

Hall, Jane

  Every quilter's foundation piecing reference tool : easy-to-use, step-by-step basics--adapt any block for foundation piecing--techniques, tips & tricks--bonus 73 blocks / Jane Hall & Dixie Haywood.

    p. cm.

  Summary: "This accessible guide shows how to employ the most-used foundation techniques for any pieced block"--Provided by publisher.

  ISBN 978-1-57120-590-2 (paper trade : alk. paper)

  1. Patchwork--Patterns. 2. Quilting--Patterns. I. Haywood, Dixie. II. Title.

  TT835.H22185 2009

  746.46--dc22

                          2008037140

Printed in China

10 9 8 7 6 5 4 3 2 1

Contents

Introduction

Our aim in writing this accessible guide was to show readers how they could employ the most-used foundation techniques for any pieced block, either in its original form or with slight adaptations.

We have divided blocks into categories that lead to logical divisions and the use of the most efficient foundation technique—or, in some cases, more than one technique. As you examine the blocks, paying attention to the divisions and techniques used, we hope you will learn how to "read" other blocks for piecing in this faster and more precise way of working.

Our resources for the majority of the blocks were *The Encyclopedia of Pieced Quilt Patterns* by Barbara Brackman (hard copy and electronic versions) and Electric Quilt software. Both sources contain many more delightful blocks than we were able to include in our limited space. We hope this book will inspire you to explore those blocks with an eye to piecing them on foundations.

# The Basics

Piecing on a foundation has become a boon to quiltmakers of all levels of expertise. A foundation is any material that you stitch *on* or *with* to provide stability and precision. This old-made-new technique uses an extra element in the piecing process and is an easily mastered approach to quiltmaking.

ADVANTAGES

Stabilization: This was the original use of foundations. A foundation can stabilize the stitching together of fabrics of many different weights and weaves. Fabric stretches, and seamed pieces have enormous potential to lose shape, especially when bias edges are involved.

Precision: A foundation gives total accuracy when piecing and joining patches, blocks, and borders.

Efficiency and speed: The need for templates is reduced or totally eliminated.

Design aid: Piecing order and color placement can be noted directly on the foundation, streamlining construction and reducing errors.

FOUNDATION TYPES

A **permanent foundation** of fabric or interfacing remains in the piece. A **temporary foundation**, made of various types of papers or removable interfacing, is torn out when the piecing is complete.

The choice of foundation is often influenced by the type of quilt—bed, wall, or wearable; the kind of quilting or embellishment planned; and the availability of material. Lightweight foundations are often the best choice. Many papers and interfacings are translucent, which is also desirable.

FOUNDATION MATERIALS

Permanent

Fabric: Fabric can act as interfacing for clothing and gives stability to machine quilting. It adds bulk when hand quilting. Match the weight of the foundation fabric to the project. Fabric should be preshrunk.

Interfacing: Has the same qualities as fabric. Do not use bias interfacing.

Flannel: This can be used as a combination foundation and filler. Flannel should be preshrunk.

Batting or fleece: This material can be used to piece and quilt in one step. Be sure to use it with fabric backing to avoid distortion.

Temporary

Tracing paper: This paper is translucent, easy to mark, and easy to remove. However, it may tear prematurely.

Tear-away interfacing: Like tracing paper, this is a translucent material. It is less likely to tear prematurely. It can also act as a permanent foundation.

Vellum tracing paper: Although this is more expensive than interfacing or tracing paper, it is less likely to tear prematurely.

Examining room table paper: Similar to tracing paper, this inexpensive paper is especially useful when a long foundation is needed.

Freezer paper: Freezer paper is good for difficult-to-control fabric or when a long foundation is needed. However, it is more difficult to remove when pressed repeatedly, and it is not as pliable as some materials. Use the shiny side against fabric.

Adhesive paper: This paper, which adheres well, is good for single foundations sewn by hand or machine. *Do not iron* as it melts with heat.

Preprinted foundations: Many patterns are available on preprinted foundations in pads or sheets.

Typing or photocopy paper: This is not the best option, as it is not translucent and it may tear prematurely. You also must use very small machine stitches to avoid distortion when it is removed.

MARKING THE FOUNDATION

Most of the techniques require you to mark the pattern on the foundation. Your choice of marking techniques may depend on the foundation material you're using or what you have available. Either way, there is a wide variety from which to choose.

Before you begin, you will need to decide the piecing order for sewing the patches and then mark that information on the foundation. Some blocks have options for the first piece. Other patterns have only one possible starting place. You also must decide whether the foundation will be the finished size of the block or will include a ¼″ seam allowance on all sides. Including the seam allowance in the foundation can provide more stability, but doing so requires picking out the small bits of foundation from the seam allowance.

Marking Tools and Techniques

Tracing: When tracing, use a thin-lead pencil and a transparent ruler for accuracy. Tracing is tedious for multiples but useful for a quick sample block. Avoid pens, which may transfer to fabric when pressed.

Computer printing or digital copy based on a scanned image: This produces very accurate images. Be sure to use the thinnest paper your printer will handle.

Hot iron transfer: This technique is good for marking multiple copies on fabric. Use a transfer pencil to make a hot iron transfer. Sharpen the pencil often to keep a consistent point when drawing the transfer.

Stamps and stencils: Many patterns of stamps and stencils are available. Most are small and traditional. Many office supply companies can make a custom stamp.

Tracing wheel: With the use of dressmaker's carbon paper, multiple copies can be made using a dressmaker's tracing wheel on paper or fabric.

Photocopy: Avoid photocopying if possible. Even the best machine can distort the image, usually in only one direction, making a slightly rectangular block. If you must photocopy, always use the original. Never copy a copy.

Needle punch: This is our favorite method for making accurate multiple foundations on paper. The process results in a neat stack of identical patterns, firmly held together by the punching of the sewing machine. All kinds of paper can be needle punched; tracing paper is especially suitable. However, this technique does not work well for fabric or interfacing, because the holes are not visible.

1. Unthread your sewing machine, both top and bobbin.

2. Pin a pattern onto a stack of up to 12 sheets of lightweight paper. Staple or use a few pins to anchor the stack together.

3. Beginning in the middle of the pattern, stitch on all the lines in one plane. Stitch on the remaining lines in that plane, then all the remaining lines in the block, including the outside lines.

Needle punching a stack of paper

4. Check on the back of the stack of patterns to make sure you have sewn on all lines.

5. If you want the foundations to be the finished size, trim the excess paper on the outside block lines, leaving a small tab on one corner to make it easy to separate the pages.

A tab to help separate the papers

tip

If you are needle punching freezer paper, the waxy side will slip easily against the feed dogs. To fool the feed dogs, position a piece of fabric under the stack of paper. The needle punching will then be quick and easy.

The Techniques

There are three basic techniques using foundations, plus several variations within these techniques. In these examples, the foundation is the finished size.

TOP PRESSED PIECING

Top pressed piecing is the oldest of the techniques, used first in the United States in the latter half of the nineteenth century for Log Cabin patterns. It was also used for the Pineapple, a Log Cabin variation, and later for crazy piecing and string designs. The latter two create appealing designs by themselves and add texture to blocks, backgrounds, and borders.

Sample Block: Diagonal String

1. Pin the first fabric piece to the foundation, right side up. Pin the second piece facedown on the first, matching cut edges.

Pin the first pieces to the foundation.

2. Stitch on the fabric through all layers, using a ¼″ seam allowance.

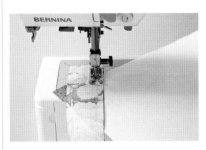

Stitching the second piece to the first

3. Open the second piece and press against the foundation. Pin in place. Repeat Steps 2 and 3 until the foundation is covered with fabric.

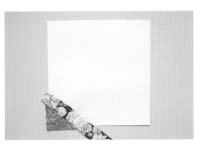

Second piece opened and pinned to the foundation.

4. Press the block flat and trim the excess seam allowance to ¼″.

Trimming the finished block

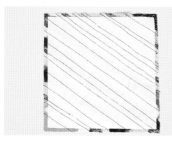

Back of finished block

Finished block

If you use irregularly shaped pieces of fabric and strips with this technique, it becomes crazy piecing, which provides even more texture.

Crazy-pieced block

UNDER PRESSED PIECING

This technique was devised in the 1980s by several quilt teachers in an attempt to more accurately piece Log Cabin and Pineapple designs. After the pattern is drawn on the foundation, fabric pieces are pinned to the *undrawn*, or top, side of the foundation. The foundation is turned over so the fabric rests against the feed dogs. The stitching is then done directly on the drawn lines on the other side of the foundation.

Sample Block: Sailboat

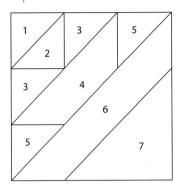

Sailboat block

This block, often shown as a single block, is also interesting as a rotated quarter of a larger design (see page 44).

1. Place the first piece on the undrawn side of the foundation, right side up, overlapping the drawn line by ¼″. Place the second piece right side down on top of the first, matching cut edges. Pin, taking care to position the pin out of the stitching line.

The first two pieces pinned in place

2. Stitch on the line, beginning and ending a stitch or two beyond each end of the line.

Sewing on the line

3. Open the second piece, pressing it flat against the foundation, taking care not to form a pleat. Pin and keep the pin in place until the next round.

Second piece opened and pinned to the foundation

Piece pinned open in the seam allowance

4. Turn to the marked side, fold the foundation on the next sewing line, and trim any excess fabric to ¼" to form an accurate placement line for the next patch.

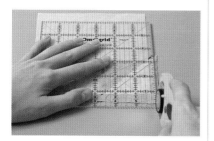

Trimming excess seam allowance

5. Continue adding pieces, pinning, stitching, and trimming as before, until the foundation is covered. Press the block flat and trim the outside seam allowance to ¼".

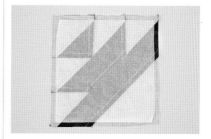

Back of finished block

Finished Sailboat block

This is the technique of choice for most foundation piecing today. It creates accurate points and allows blocks to be joined with precision.

Strip piecing is simple and virtually trouble free with under pressed piecing. In conventional strip piecing, strips are sewn into sets and then crosscut into slices or shapes. These long seams sometimes wobble, however, making the slices inexact. Instead, sew the strip set to a freezer paper foundation to eliminate that inaccuracy.

Draw lines at the desired intervals on freezer paper. Use under pressed piecing to add the strips in order, pressing firmly after each seam. Depending on the pattern, cut the strip set into slices or shapes (which can be drawn first on the paper), then assemble the block.

This is a good technique for parts of blocks or for entire designs.

Strip set with one triangle cut off

Mock Log Cabin made from strip set

SINGLE FOUNDATION PIECING

Single foundation piecing is a direct descendant of English paper piecing, in which each patch of fabric in the block has its own template or foundation. Instead of hand basting fabric to paper shapes, use freezer paper and iron the shapes to the wrong side of fabric. You can piece by hand or machine to stitch the patches together along the edge of the templates.

Sample Block: The Pansy

The Pansy is an example of one of the pieced flower/animal designs that is made more accessible with this technique. Although some portions of the block could be made using *under* pressed piecing, it is just as easy to use single foundations for the entire block, with the added benefit of controlling seam allowance directions.

1. Draw the pattern on the dull side of freezer paper. Code the pieces, marking the grainline and color choices on the foundation.

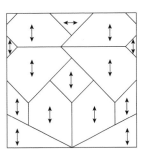

Pansy block with grainline marked

2. Cut the foundation apart on the lines and press the pieces onto the wrong side of the fabrics. Cut out the shapes, adding ¼″ seam allowance on all sides.

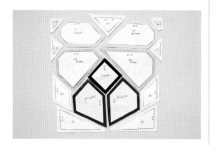

Press foundations onto fabric and cut out shapes.

tip Draw an extra pattern to use as a reference. Either mark the coding on it or pin the prepared foundations to it as a construction aid.

3. Reassemble the pattern, matching the cut edges of the freezer paper as you pin pieces together. Aim for long straight seams, although set-in seams can be sewn in two steps, stopping and starting at the end of each seam. Press seams open.

Assemble the pieces.

tip Do not stitch across seamlines where there is an inset seam. Insert the sewing machine needle at the exact beginning of the sewing line, backstitching at both ends of the seam.

Finished block

This technique is often used for pictorial blocks, as well as for patterns containing hexagons and diamonds. It is also frequently found in combination with pressed piecing in blocks that cannot be completely press pieced.

The Formats

In the past, pressed piecing was used only for whole blocks because of the geometric limitation requiring that the next piece added must be a long, straight line. You cannot pivot or set-in a seam as you can with ordinary seam-to-seam piecing.

The solution to this problem is to divide the block into straight-edged segments at the points where pressed piecing cannot continue. Each segment can then be press pieced and joined to other segments, using the foundation edges as guides. Some segments may be *single* or even conventional nonfoundation piecing. This technique retains the stability and precision of whole-block foundation piecing, and potentially opens the entire lexicon of pieced patterns to this type of piecing, whether using one foundation technique or a combination of several.

Similar-looking blocks may have to be divided differently.

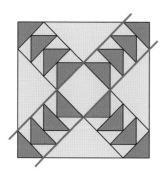
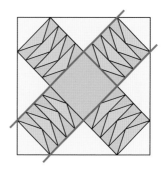

Goose in the Pond   Wild Goose Chase

Goose in the Pond uses only three segments. Wild Goose Chase requires four segments, because of the orientation of the large "goose" triangles.

CHOICES

There may be more than one way to divide the block, as well as more than one technique to use to piece it. Be creative and figure out the way that is fastest and easiest for you.

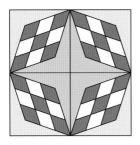

Four Block Star, original

The Four Block Star is a fairly complicated block that can be pieced on foundations in several different ways.

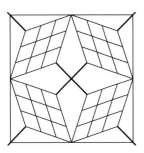

Four Block Star, version 1

Eliminate the seams in the center of the star and draw diagonal lines through both the star and the outer corners. The large diamonds can be sewn with strip piecing or *under* press piecing on three foundations for each diamond. The remaining pieces will be single foundations.

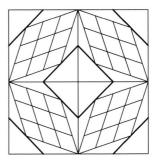

Four Block Star, version 2

Draw a square on point in the center and then echo the same lines in the corners. Piece the diamonds as for version 1 and use single foundations for the remaining pieces.

The blocks will be identical, but the center star will have different seams . . . your choice.

tip

Any block can be entirely pieced using single foundation piecing. Some quiltmakers do just that for control of both the fabric print and the direction of the seam allowances. As a rule, however, pressed piecing is more efficient, quick, and accurate because you don't spend as much time matching edges and pinning.

EXAMINING A BLOCK

When you select a block, consider the following questions as you decide how to piece it:

- Are there advantages to piecing this block on a foundation, either completely or partially?

- Which piecing technique will work best? Pressed (*top* or *under*), *single* foundation, or a combination of techniques?

- Which format should be used? Whole block? Segments?

- If segments are used, what is the most efficient division of the block? Diagonal?

Horizontal? Asymmetric? Investigate different divisions to see which works best. How many segments should be used? What is the piecing order?

- Would the block benefit from adjustment of some lines? Adding or subtracting lines can make piecing easier or can enhance the graphics or fabric design.

tip
Segment division may be determined by the piecing format or technique you prefer.

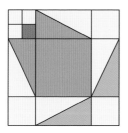

Magnolia Bud

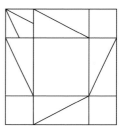

Magnolia Bud, altered: By changing the tip, you get not only a more pleasing design but also a simpler design to piece.

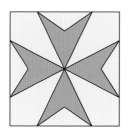

Four Petals

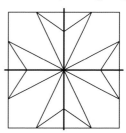

Four Petals, altered: Adding horizontal and vertical seams makes this much easier to piece on foundations.

GETTING STARTED

Once you have chosen a block:

1. Select a technique.

2. Choose the foundation material.

3. Trace the block onto the foundation, marking the divisions and coding the piecing order.

4. Cut the foundation into segments.

5. Cut fabric for the patches.

tip

If the pattern is asymmetric, it is *very* important that you mark the front or top of the foundation segments to ensure that piecing is always done on the same side of the foundation.

Cutting Fabric

Pressed piecing requires a slightly larger seam allowance for the sewn and flipped-open piece to adequately cover the appropriate space. The first piece should have an accurate ¼" seam allowance for accurate placement of the initial pieces. We suggest ⅜" for subsequent pieces. Although this will probably require trimming after stitching to create an accurate placement line for the next piece to be added, it will solve the problem of pieces not covering the space adequately.

Strips or squares: Cut a full ¼" seam allowance.

tip

Cutting half and quarter-square triangles, depending on their orientation in the block, not only controls stretch by keeping the outer edge of the block on the straight of grain, but also aligns grainline and print in the same direction, creating a more pleasing block.

Half-square triangles: To make quick-cut right-angle triangles, add 1¼" to the measurement of the side of a right-angle triangle. Make a square with that measurement and cut it in half on the diagonal. Each triangle will have a ⅜" seam allowance, and the sides of the triangle will be on grain.

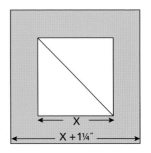

Half-square triangles

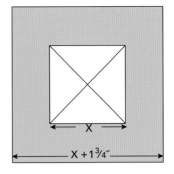

Quarter-square triangles

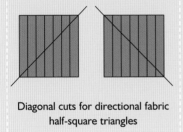
Quarter-square triangles: To make quarter-square triangles, add 1¾″ to the measurement of the long side of the right-angle triangle. Make a square with that measurement and cut the square on both diagonals, creating four triangles, each with a ⅜″ seam allowance. The long side will be on grain.

Other shapes: For other shapes, including triangles and polygons, make a *cutting* template of the finished shape as a guide to cut fabric with appropriate seam allowances. We suggest that you make an extra copy of the segment that you can cut up and use as templates for cutting fabric. If you use freezer paper, you can press the templates on top of several layers of fabric for easy cutting. Remember that the first patch on any segment should have ¼″ seam allowances, and the subsequent patches ⅜″ seam allowances on all sides.

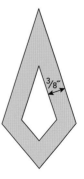

Cutting template

Mirror Image

With *under* pressed piecing, you will be working in a reverse image, because the pattern is drawn on one side of the foundation and the fabric is placed on the opposite side. In an asymmetric design, if the direction or slant of the pattern piece is important, place the fabric on the drawn side of the foundation and stitch on the undrawn side to avoid sewing a reversed pattern.

Depending on the pattern, you may be cutting fabric in different ways. For a design with mirror symmetry within the pattern, cut the fabric folded to create mirror image pieces. Other patterns may require cutting patches singly to accommodate the direction of the shapes.

If you are going to sew on the *drawn* side of the foundation, as is customary, place the cutting templates on the *wrong* side of the fabrics so that the angles of the shapes will match the drawn pattern. Correspondingly, if you are going to stitch on the *undrawn* side of the foundation (in order not to reverse the orientation of the pattern), place the cutting templates on the *right* side of the fabric. The latter assumes you are using a translucent foundation, on which the lines are visible on the undrawn side.

With *single* foundation piecing, you also work in mirror image. However, because each template is placed individually on the wrong side of the fabric, there is less opportunity for confusion in fabric cutting.

CONSTRUCTION

Regardless of the technique you are using, take time to prepare the foundations, cut the fabrics, and go through the necessary steps to stitch and join the segments. These are win-win techniques, but, as always, they are dependent on the care and skill of the quiltmaker.

Stitching

Stitching on foundations can be done by hand or by machine, though temporary foundations are more easily sewn by machine. The added foundation layer requires a smaller-than-usual stitch length to keep stitches tight and to keep them from distorting when the foundations are eventually torn out. For lightweight foundations, we recommend 15 stitches per inch, or 1.75 metric. (For heavier foundations, use 22 stitches per inch, or 1.5 metric.)

Construction Tips

- When you have a choice between beginning to press piece at a corner or beginning in a center, consider control of the seam allowances (and subsequent quilting designs). The seam allowances will fold under the second piece.

- When adding patches around a center patch, sew opposite sides to ensure the integrity of the center.

- Sew *into* (rather than beginning at) tricky points for better control of the seamline. This is true for long, skinny points as well as for places where multiple seams cross.

- When piecing a block with repeated strips, begin piecing at opposite ends of alternate segments. When the segments are joined, the seams will face opposite directions and fit together snugly.

- Before beginning to piece, lay out the segments as they are positioned in the finished block, making sure that the foundations are all the same side up. If you have precut fabric pieces, keep the cutting templates on top of the piles of patches to identify them.

- The easiest way to ensure that you are positioning a patch properly is to place it right side up on the foundation *just as it will look when finished*. Then flip it over, matching the cut edges to the under piece, and stitch.

Joining Segments and Blocks

1. Press the completed segments *firmly*. Work from the fabric side first, pressing away from the seam so the fabric is flat with no pleats or wrinkles. Then press from the foundation side. This will help the accuracy of the joining points.

tip

When the outer pieces of fabric in the finished block are not anchored by cross seams, keep them flat and accurately placed on the foundation by sewing a few long basting stitches across each patch. Remove the basting after you join the segments.

2. For accuracy and to keep both segment edges aligned during sewing, it is important to pin adequately at each corner, at each joining point within the seam, and along the seamlines.

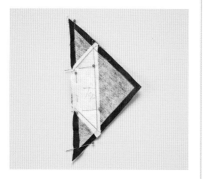

Pin pieces together.

3. Stab pins at the joining points. Before stitching, fold back the seam allowances and check that the points and lines match perfectly. If the seams are angled, the joining point should form a perfect chevron.

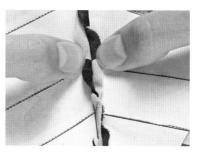

Check the chevron.

4. Because you are joining two segments with foundations against the feed dogs, the assembly will be a little more slippery than fabric alone would be. Sew slowly, removing pins as you go and carefully guiding the sewing machine needle.

5. Press the seams open to reduce bulk and retain the precise points.

THE BLOCKS

For the following blocks, unless otherwise specified, use *under* pressed piecing. Remember that this technique is only as accurate as your ability to sew on the line. Unless otherwise noted, when using cutting templates you should cut with the fabric folded, producing two mirror image pieces.

Numbering: The same numbers on matching pieces indicate that it does not matter which is sewn first, because they both are sewn before the next numbered patches are added. For some of the complex blocks with identical segments, not all segments are numbered; simply repeat the order of the marked segment. Single foundations are identified with the word *single* or an encircled S.

WHOLE BLOCKS

Whole block patterns were originally stitched by hand on fabric foundations. Piecing may start in the center, at the top, or at a corner. Many whole blocks are more interesting in multiples, where they often create strong graphics and new secondary patterns.

Square on Square

 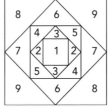

This classic block is effective in fabrics with good contrast between the rows.

Fabric cutting: Squares; half-square and quarter-square triangles

Four Mosaic blocks

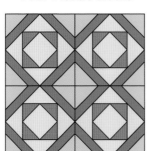

This block is similar to Square on Square but with strips on the outer corners, creating a framed secondary design when multiple blocks are joined.

Virginia Reel

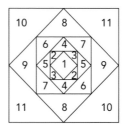

This old favorite has many names and variations.

Fabric cutting: Squares; half-square and quarter-square triangles

Mark the colors on the foundation to avoid confusion during piecing.

Sweet Gum Leaf

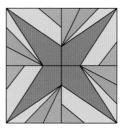

Four Sweet Gum Leaf blocks

This block has a contemporary look forming a large star with
secondary designs when four blocks are rotated 90° and joined.

Fabric cutting: Cutting templates for all shapes to ensure accurate
angles of the odd-shaped patches

Begin piecing with the center patch to make the seam allowances on the
center star uniform.

Roman Stripe

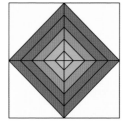

Four Roman Stripe blocks

This classic pattern offers several different piecing options: *under* pressed piecing in four
segments, strip piecing on a foundation, or *top* pressed piecing using random strips.

Fabric cutting: Strips; half-square triangles

Milky Way

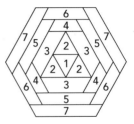

This hybrid of the Log Cabin and Pineapple patterns has great graphic effects.

 Fabric cutting: Strips; cutting templates for center shape

Pineapple

Four Pineapple blocks

For this old favorite Log Cabin variation, it is easy
to keep all the strips even on a foundation.

Fabric cutting: Strips; squares

HALF DIVISIONS

These blocks align on either a horizontal/vertical or diagonal axis,
depending on the design and the piecing order. The halves can be identical or mirror symmetric; in some cases, the halves need to
be reversed to complete the design.

Dutchman's Puzzle

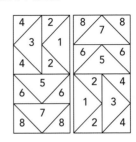

This block and the next two (Indian Emblem and Return of the Swallows)
use identical patches with different coloration. Each half of this block
is identical, and one must be reversed to create the pattern.

 Fabric cutting: Half-square and quarter-square triangles

Indian Emblem   Return of the Swallows

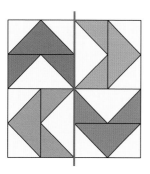
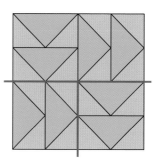

Although these have identical shapes and fabric cutting as the
Dutchman's Puzzle, the orientation of the patches requires different divisions.

Chinese Lanterns

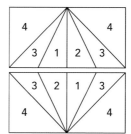

This square block has a diamond focus.

Fabric cutting: Half-square triangles; cutting templates

Begin piecing in the middle of the segments for control of the seam
allowances.

Perpetual Motion

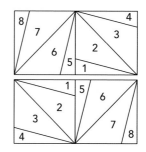

This block indeed has motion, and in multiples, it creates
interesting tessellations with secondary star designs.

Fabric cutting: Cutting templates for all shapes on single layers
of fabric

Star of Spring

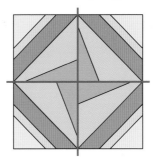

This block is similar to Perpetual Motion. As shown, it must be pieced in four segments. If the points of the star were extended to the edge, it could be pieced in two segments.

 Fabric cutting: Strips; half-square triangles; cutting templates on single layers of fabric

Left and Right

 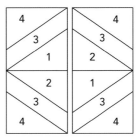

This contemporary-looking block offers simple piecing and interesting color play when multiples are joined.

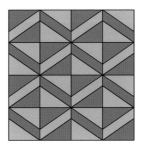

Four Left and Right blocks

Fabric cutting: Strips; cutting templates for the triangles

Chevrons

 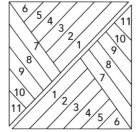

This graphic block can be pieced in two segments with *under* pressed piecing or in four segments using strip sets. An interesting alternative might be random *top* pressed piecing.

When rotated and flipped, multiples of the block create dynamic secondary designs (16 blocks shown).

 Fabric cutting: Strips

Mrs. Taft's Choice

 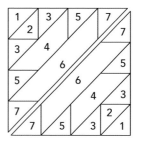

This block is effective in several different sets: side by side, rotated, or even sashed. To piece it as a half-block, divide the two corner squares of the traditional version diagonally.

 Fabric cutting: Strips; half-square triangles

Allentown

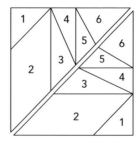

A strange, single block, this one offers a good opportunity for color play.

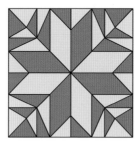

Multiple Allentown blocks come to life when you rotate them.

Fabric cutting: Half-square triangles; cutting templates

The Palm

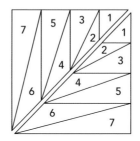

This traditional pattern has challenging sharp points.

Fabric cutting: Cutting templates for all shapes

Carefully pin the joining points of the two halves.

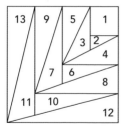

If the print of the fabric is not an issue, lines within the pattern can be altered, which will allow it to be pieced as a whole block, avoiding the somewhat demanding assembly of two halves.

The Palm, altered

QUARTER DIVISIONS

Blocks can be divided into quarters on either the vertical and horizontal lines or on the diagonal lines. The segments can be identical, mirror imaged, offset, or rotated to create the final block.

Horizontal or Vertical Divisions

Aircraft

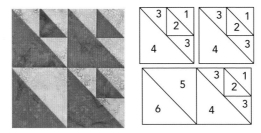

This block can be divided evenly into four segments, two of which can be combined to make it a three-segment block.

Fabric cutting: Half-square triangles in two sizes

Blacks and Whites

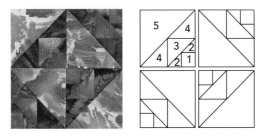

This is a curious name for a block that has many color options. Rotated segments create the pattern, and multiples make several secondary patterns.

Fabric cutting: Squares; half-square and quarter-square triangles in several sizes

Rosebud

 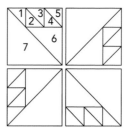

This old-fashioned block with simple sawtooth
elements is not as complicated as it looks.

Fabric cutting: Half-square triangles in two sizes

Pinwheel 2

 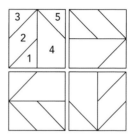

This double pinwheel has good movement.
Mark the colors on the foundations for piecing ease.

Fabric cutting: Strips; half-square triangles; cutting templates

New Jersey

 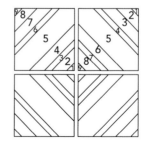

This dynamic block may be pieced in four segments using *under* pressed
piecing, but it is an ideal block for strip piecing using strips sets.

Fabric cutting: Strips in several sizes

Diagonal Divisions

Many blocks divide evenly into four diagonal segments.

Turnstile

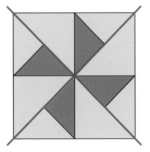

Diagonal segments make this piecing simple.

Tilted Turnstile

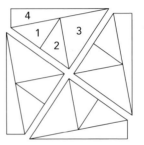

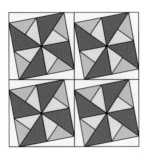

In this dynamic version of the Turnstile block, stars are formed by joining four blocks.

Fabric cutting: Half-square and quarter-square triangles; cutting templates for corner shapes

Pinwheel I

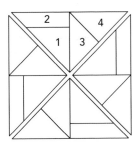

This is a simple version of several blocks that have the same name.

Fabric cutting: Strips; half-square and quarter-square triangles

Jewel

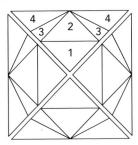

Add diagonal lines through the corner pieces to make an easily pieced four-segment block. In the original version, without the added lines, the construction would be a combination of *under* pressed piecing and set-in single foundations.

Fabric cutting: Quarter-square triangles; cutting templates

Star and Dot

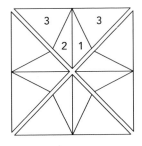

This block shows a prominent star in a simple setting.

Fabric cutting: Cutting templates for all shapes

Broken Spider Web

 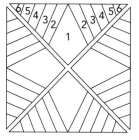

This is a good block for color gradations. *Under* pressed piecing could be used for the entire block or only for the center star. *Top* pressed piecing would give a more random appearance to the design.

Multiples of this block create circles
and waves of color.

 Fabric cutting: Strips; cutting templates for center shape

Riviera

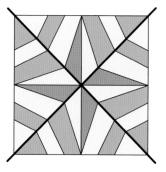

This is a wild combination of the Star and Dot
and Broken Spider Web blocks.

Key West Beauty

 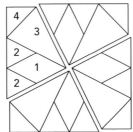

This Kaleidoscope block variation has uneven quadrants.

Fabric cutting: Half-square triangles; cutting templates

Block Island Puzzle

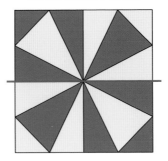

This Kaleidoscope block variation looks as if it should be divided further, but the position of the shapes allows for just two segments.

Flora's Favorite

 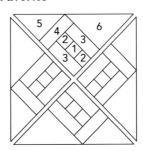

The interior piecing is a Log Cabin variation. For this block, you need to be aware of the mirror image effect. To keep the letters from being reversed, place the fabrics on the *drawn* side of the foundation and stitch on the other side.

Fabric cutting: Strips; quarter-square triangles

Starry Path

 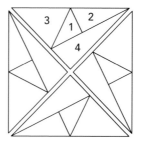

This dynamic block requires careful planning and marking in order for the colors to weave properly. Mark the colors on the foundation before cutting it apart into segments.

Fabric cutting: Cutting templates for all shapes on single layers of fabric—corresponding patches in each segment are identical

Unnamed Star

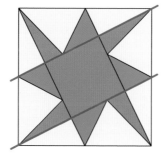

This relative of Starry Path is much more easily pieced.

EIGHTH DIVISIONS

This division makes precise piecing of more-complex blocks easy. Blocks divided into eighths usually use diagonal and angled lines, and the segments may not be identical.

Featherbone

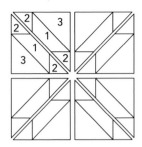

Simple divisions make a complex-appearing design.

Fabric cutting: Strips; half-square triangles

Hunter's Star

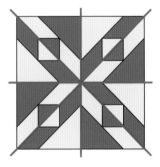

This block is similar to Featherbone but with an additional design element.

Twisting Star

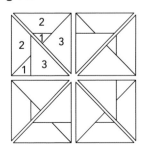

Reminiscent of Card Trick, this block requires careful color marking on the foundations. Mitered corner lines were added to the original block to echo the diagonal design lines.

Fabric cutting: Strips; half-square and quarter-square triangles

Wheel of Fortune

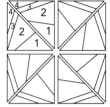

This block is a dressed-up pinwheel design.

A framed star is formed by joining four blocks.

Fabric cutting: Strips; cutting templates

Blazing Star

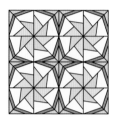
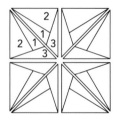

This classic favorite has great color play. Mark the colors on foundations to avoid confusion when piecing.

Fabric cutting: Cutting templates for all shapes

Spider Web

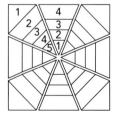

Using *under* pressed piecing and alternating the piecing direction in each segment allows you to easily match and join the seams. This block could be strip pieced using two strip sets and would also be fun with random *top* pressed piecing.

Fabric cutting: Strips

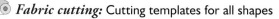

tip

Press each strip firmly from the seamline out, so the seamlines are sharp and easy to match.

Target

 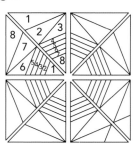

This block has great graphics. One option is to drop the extra piecing in the lower right corner to create an additional design when blocks are joined. Alternating the direction of the piecing in each segment allows you to easily match and join the seams.

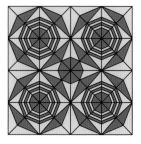

In multiples, the graphics are even more stunning.

Fabric cutting: Strips; cutting templates

Double Star

 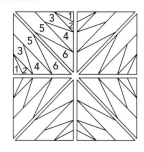

This complex block is easily pieced on foundations. Take care to mark the colors on the foundation before cutting it apart.

Fabric cutting: Cutting templates for all shapes

EVEN DIVISIONS

Some blocks divide—either horizontally or vertically—into three, four, five, or even seven straight rows as segments.

Double X

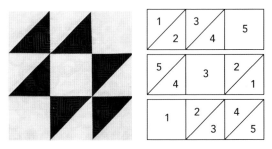

Depending on the coloration, this block can look like a flock of birds or like double Xs.

Fabric cutting: Squares; half-square triangles

Dove at the Window

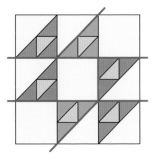

This block has the same shapes as Double X but is more interesting and has more segments because of the interior piecing.

Illinois

 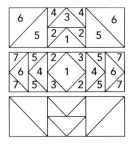

Another nine-patch, but this time it is divided into three equal rows/segments.

Fabric cutting: Squares; half-square triangles in two sizes; quarter-square triangles

Colt's Corral

 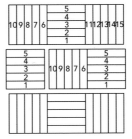

This block has an interesting woven effect and can be done with strip sets as well as with *under* pressed piecing.

 Fabric cutting: Strips

Single Wedding Ring

 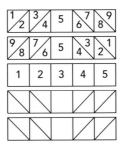

This easy block for a special occasion is pieced in 5 rows. Alternating the direction of piecing in each segment allows you to easily match and join the seams.

 Fabric cutting: Squares; half-square triangles

ASYMMETRIC DIVISIONS

Many blocks require division into uneven segments. Don't give up on foundation piecing for blocks that at first don't seem to fall into obvious segment divisions.

Rambler

 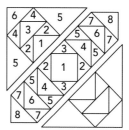

Only three segments are needed in this block because of the orientation of the triangles.

Fabric cutting: Squares; half-square and quarter-square triangles

Delaware Crosspatch

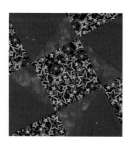 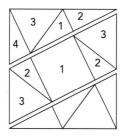

This unusual block, which appears to be spinning, is easily divided into only three segments.

Fabric cutting: Squares; cutting templates

Combination Star

 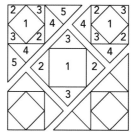

This variation of the Ohio Star with many matching points is a no-brainer for foundation piecing using five segments.

Fabric cutting: Squares; half-square and quarter-square triangles

Broken Dishes

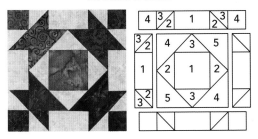

This is a simple, five-segment division of a basketlike design. Be sure to mark the colors on the foundation before cutting it apart.

Fabric cutting: Squares; half-square and quarter-square triangles; rectangles

Capital T

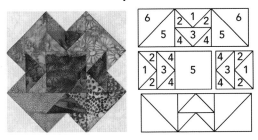

One of the more interesting "letter" blocks, this one is divided into four segments.

Fabric cutting: Squares; half-square and quarter-square triangles

Crossroads

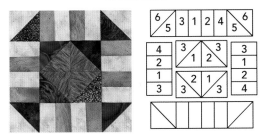

This block offers a choice of foundation techniques. The center can be divided into two segments, or the cross seams can be dropped out to create one segment. The outer segment can be made with *under* pressed piecing or strip piecing. Note the piecing order for the rectangles; this forms identical seam allowances in the end triangles.

Fabric cutting: Strips; half-square triangles

Mother's Favorite

This variation of the Sailboat block (page 11) has an added center square.
The four corner segments are joined to the center segment.
The final seams are easily sewn with short miters.

Four Sailboat blocks

Fabric cutting: Strips; squares; half-square and quarter-square triangles

The Airplane

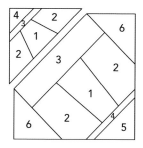

This representational design is easily divided into segments.

Fabric cutting: Strips; half-square triangles; cutting templates

Card Trick

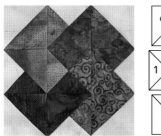
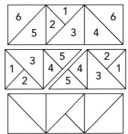

Both this block and the Gray Goose (below) are divided into four segments, with odd-shaped center segments, to accommodate the many cross seams. Both require careful marking of colors on the foundations.

Gray Goose

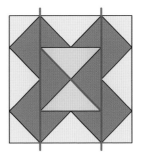

Fabric cutting: Half-square and quarter-square triangles in several sizes

Jack in the Box

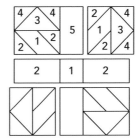

In blocks with sashing through the center, there are several options for dividing into segments. Avoid setting in the center square.

Fabric cutting: Strips; squares; half-square triangles

Crazy Ann

 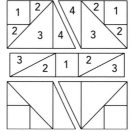

In this block, the center sashing becomes part of the design.

 Fabric cutting: Squares; half-square triangles; half-rectangle triangles cut on single layers of fabric

tip

Half-rectangle triangles can be quick-cut from rectangles using the same technique that is used for half-square triangles but adding 2″ to the long side and 1″ to the short side. Make a rectangle following these measurements and cut it on the diagonal to make identical long triangles. If designs call for mirror image triangles, cut the rectangles from folded fabric.

Dogtooth Violet

 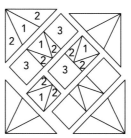

In this pretty block, precise points matter.

Fabric cutting: Squares; cutting templates, half-rectangle triangles (Diagonal rectangles can be quick-cut to make the triangles, but they must be mirror imaged. See Crazy Ann tip, above.)

Thorny Thicket

 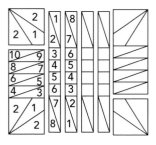

This block requires a lot of close matching. Although the center could be pieced from strip sets, *under* pressed piecing is more efficient. Alternating the direction of piecing in each segment allows you to easily match and join the seams. The long skinny triangles can be cut either with cutting templates or with half-rectangles.

Fabric cutting: Strips or squares; cutting templates

Star and Crown

 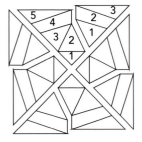

Sometimes it is necessary to be more inventive than just creating square, triangular, or rectangular segments. Dividing this block into irregular segments allows it to be completely and easily press pieced.

Fabric cutting: Strips; quarter-square triangles; cutting templates

Delectable Mountains

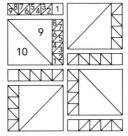

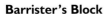

Each quarter-block has two segments. The design looks complicated, but taken one step at a time, it is easy and very precise.

Fabric cutting: Squares; half-square triangles in two sizes

Barrister's Block

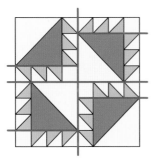

Kansas Troubles

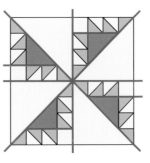

Both Kansas Troubles and Barrister's Block use the same piecing system as Delectable Mountains, with either two or three segments in each quarter.

The Chief

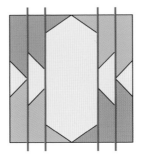

The Chief 2

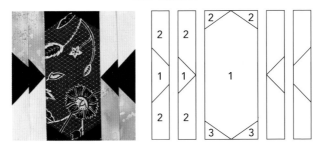

This rare block has great graphics when multiple blocks are rotated and joined. The side segments are quickly pieced with chain piecing. Reversing the side sections in the original version creates a better design for multiples.

Four the Chief 2 blocks

Fabric cutting: Strips; quarter-square triangles; cutting templates

SINGLE FOUNDATION PIECING

This foundation technique can be easily pieced either by hand or by machine. It can be used for the complete block or for portions of the block. There are no fabric-cutting directions because freezer paper templates are pressed directly onto the fabric for all shapes.

tip

Many of the seams using single templates are set-in seams, so it is important not to sew across the seam allowances. Backstitch exactly at the beginning and end points of each seam.

Eight-Pointed Star

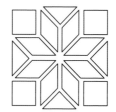

Using single templates for the entire block is a highly effective way to piece this popular pattern.

LeMoyne Star Variations

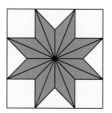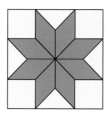

These blocks are identical to the Eight-Pointed Star, but with split or alternate points. These star points can also be made with strip piecing or with random string or crazy-pieced *top* pressed piecing.

tip

For the best effect, cut the diamonds with the grainline running from point to point.

A different but successful way to construct these stars is to sew a background triangle or square to the same side of each diamond star point. Then join the segments from the center of the diamonds out, in both directions. Stitch the final joining seam in two steps from the center to the outer edge.

Job's Troubles

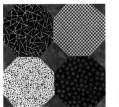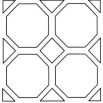

This is a great block for a scrap quilt. Although it contains many set-in seams, the angles are easy.

Wonder of Egypt

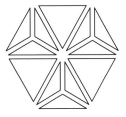

An unusual hexagon-based design, this block is rarely seen.

Mosaic Flower

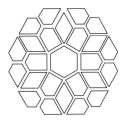

These variations of the hexagon pattern are made more interesting by the addition of other shapes. Color them as flowers or shade them differently. Single blocks can be appliquéd to backgrounds, or other filler shapes can be added to join multiple blocks.

Friendship Hexagon

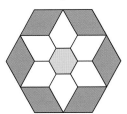

Interlocked Squares

 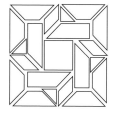

This graphic block, seldom pieced because of the many set-in seams, is easily made with single templates.

COMBINATION OF TECHNIQUES

Many blocks cannot be pieced with just one foundation technique or even entirely on foundations. Some complex designs take ingenuity to decipher the division and piecing. Although there may be many segments, the use of foundations is especially valuable for controlling points and bias edges and for ensuring that the finished block is the size planned.

tip

In blocks with pieced segments, use single foundations for the background shapes to control stretch and keep all parts of the block the same weight.

Magnolia

 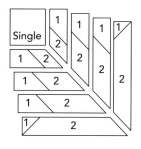

These segments are quick to complete with chain piecing. This block can be made entirely with *under* pressed piecing if the corner square is divided into two triangles, as in this example. If your fabric makes a square a better choice, use single foundation piecing for it.

Fabric cutting: Strips; half-square triangles; single foundations

Cactus Basket

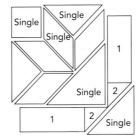

Segments in this block use single foundation piecing and both kinds of pressed piecing. The cactus segments are pieced with random *top* pressed piecing on single foundations.

Fabric cutting: Strips; half-square triangles; single foundations

Rocky Road to Kansas

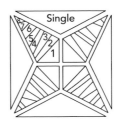

This block has a variety of good choices for piecing the star points.

- Use *top* pressed piecing for a random strip star.
- Use *under* pressed piecing for a precise strip star.
- Piece with strip sets.

These options are all pieced on single foundation segments.

Fabric cutting: Strips; half-square triangles; single foundations

Kite

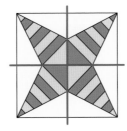

If you add a seam to each side triangle, then you can piece the block in four segments without set-in seams.

Dusty Miller

 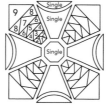

This is one of our favorite blocks, because it led us to the breakthrough idea of working on foundations in segments. The four diagonal sections use *under* pressed piecing, and the curved segments can be pieced either conventionally or with single foundations to control the bias edges. The octagon in the center is appliquéd.

Fabric cutting: Half-square triangles; cutting templates; single foundations

Mayflower

 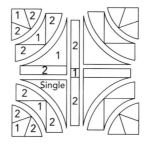

This stunning block has gentle curves. Mark the curves along the edge of the foundations; remove the foundations before piecing so you can ease the curved seams.

Fabric cutting: Strips; square; cutting templates; single foundations

Sunrise

 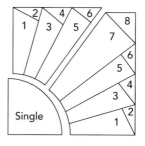

This fan design has more pizzazz than most. The curve can be pieced conventionally, with a single foundation, or appliquéd, depending on your preference.

Fabric cutting: Half-square triangle; cutting templates; single foundations

Rising Sun

 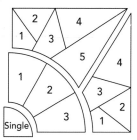

This block can be pieced in four segments, using the same options for the curved corner as were used in Sunrise (page 54).

Fabric cutting: Cutting templates; single foundations

Double Wedding Ring

This classic favorite is made simple with *under* pressed piecing for the arcs and single foundations to control the background pieces.

Fabric cutting: Strips; single foundations

Pickle Dish   ## Broken Circle

 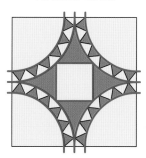

Under pressed piecing for the arcs is invaluable in these Double Wedding Ring relatives.

Pine Burr 1

 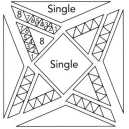

This feathered design is easily made with *under* pressed piecing and single foundations.

Fabric cutting: Half-square triangles; single foundations

Pine Burr 2

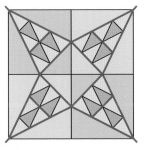

With a different orientation for the interior triangles,
this block requires different segments.

Feathered Star

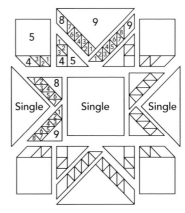

These classic favorites require many segments, some of which are oddly shaped. But controlling the points is easy and fast with foundations.

 Fabric cutting: Half-square and quarter-square triangles; single foundations

Radiant Star

tip

When examining a complex block for dividing into segments, look first for sections that will incorporate identical elements and that have straight-line piecing.

Mariner's Compass

 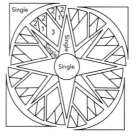

With a combination of *under* pressed piecing, single foundations, and a bit of appliqué, this stunning block will live up to its promised glory.

Fabric cutting: Cutting templates; single foundations; appliqué for center

The Rising Sun

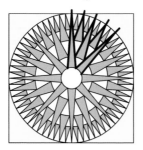

This has more segments than the Mariner's Compass but the same combination of *under* pressed piecing and single foundations.

Sunburst

 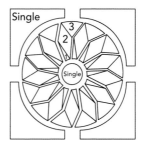

This graphic Mariner's Compass variation looks far more difficult than it is. The slightly angled segments are joined with shallow set-in seams.

Fabric cutting: Cutting templates; single foundations; appliqué for center

New York Beauty

There are many variations of this classic pattern, all with sharp, skinny points. A combination of *under* pressed piecing, single foundations, and conventional piecing allows you to neatly and easily make these points.

New York Arc

 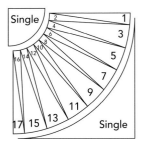

The long, skinny points—the most popular part of the New York Beauty quilt—are found in many variations of the design.

Fabric cutting: Cutting templates; single foundations

Flight of the Wild Goose

 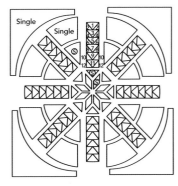

More complicated looking than it actually is, this block is easily pieced in eight Flying Geese segments, an eight-pointed star, and single foundation segments for backgrounds. The octagon with the center star was appliquéd onto the block, aligning with the rows of triangles.

Fabric cutting: Half-square and quarter-square triangles; single foundations

Moving Forward

The growing popularity of this old-made-new technique in the 1980s created many devotees of foundation piecing in all its forms. It stands to reason that new twists to the basic technique will emerge as more and more people undertake it. Bearing in mind that there is *no single right way* to work, here's a quick look at some really innovative tactics.

- **Lynn Graves** was unable to sew on the lines successfully when *under* pressed piecing and precise foundation piecing were first taught. Because she had a sewing background, she sewed an accurate ¼″ seam and realized the importance of having that marked. She invented the first ¼″ foot and began making patterns with the fabric placement line marked ¼″ beyond the seamline. For the person who has difficulty sewing "upside down and inside out"—as *under* pressed piecing has been described—Lynn's method may be the answer.

- **Judy Mathieson**, well known for her Mariner's Compass designs, found a way to avoid picking out the small bits of paper (one of the few negative aspects to foundation piecing). She folds the foundation back on the stitching line and sews exactly at the edge of the fold, giving piecers the benefit of the line without sewing through the foundation. After the block is pieced, the foundation is easily removed and can be used again.

- **Anita Grossman Solomon** uses segments *without* cutting them apart. The segments are printed ⅝″ apart on a single large vellum foundation sheet. This sheet is creased between the segments in the extra ⅛″. After using *under* pressed piecing and trimming all segments, she folds the foundation on the creases, with right sides of the pieced fabrics together, and then joins the segments. Because they were never cut apart, it is very simple to match joining lines.

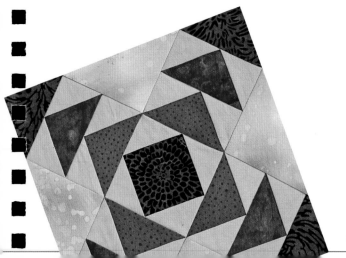

- **Cynthia England** has used *single* foundation piecing to create painterly scenes, as well as flowers and birds. She chooses to put her single templates on the *right* side of the fabric. She believes this is a forgiving technique, because it allows her to reposition the templates if they ever slip slightly.

- In a more conventional use of single foundation piecing, **Ruth McDowell** uses freezer paper templates on the wrong side of the fabric. She designs and pieces her one-of-a-kind art quilts with this technique.

Many other teachers have developed tricks and tips for foundation piecing. Numbering the piecing order on the foundations reduces confusion. Folding the foundation on the stitching line allows pretrimming of excess seam allowances from larger-than-usual patches. Computers can be used to create designs and print the segments—complete with seam allowances, if desired. An assembly-line method makes strip piecing even faster. Innovative art quilters are adapting designs for both *under* and *single* foundation techniques, demonstrating the versatility of the techniques. These novel ways of working on foundations have been documented in many books.

New tweaks continue to evolve each day. It is almost always possible to adapt a design in some way to this kind of work. And if one method doesn't entirely work for what you have in mind, you can take steps from another and make it your own.

Index

Sources

For a list of other fine books from C&T Publishing, ask for a free catalog:

C&T Publishing, Inc.
P.O. Box 1456
Lafayette, CA 94549
(800) 284-1114
Email: ctinfo@ctpub.com
Website: www.ctpub.com

C&T Publishing's professional photography services are now available to the public. Visit us at www.ctmediaservices.com.

For quilting supplies:

Cotton Patch
1025 Brown Ave.
Lafayette, CA 94549
Store: (925) 284-1177
Mail order: (925) 283-7883
Email: CottonPa@aol.com
Website: www.quiltusa.com

Note: Fabrics used in the quilts shown may not be currently available, as fabric manufacturers keep most fabrics in print for only a short time.

About the Authors

Jane Hall and Dixie Haywood are award-winning quiltmakers who are known for adapting traditional designs using contemporary techniques and innovative approaches, most often using foundation piecing. Both have been teaching and judging quiltmaking for many years, and have a strong commitment to provide students with basic fundamentals as well as creative approaches, leading to their own unique quilts. They have co-authored several books exploring Foundation Piecing, and have been called The Pineapple Queens.

Jane is a teacher, judge, and appraiser, who likes to work with traditional patterns, using innovative colorations to create new graphics. She feels almost evangelistic about foundation piecing in all its formats, especially Log Cabin, Pineapple, and Mariner's Compass patterns. She and her husband, Bob, have six grown children, many grandchildren, and live in Raleigh, North Carolina, with Tilly the calico cat.

Dixie made her first quilt in 1954 for her first child and has been quilting steadily since the late '60s. A teacher, lecturer, and quilt judge, she originally received recognition for her contemporary crazy quilts, but has always made all types of quilts, both pieced and appliquéd. She and her husband Bob have two sons, a daughter, three grandsons, and one great-granddaughter. They live in Pendleton, South Carolina, far—she hopes—from hurricanes.

Great Titles
from
C&T PUBLISHING